SUPER SANDCASTLE
Poetry Power

GUPPIES

~ TO ~

PUPPIES

Reading, Writing, and Reciting
Poems About Pets

COMPILED & EDITED BY SUSAN M. FREESE   ILLUSTRATED BY JAN WESTBERG

ABDO
Publishing Company

Published by ABDO Publishing Company, 8000 West 78th Street, Edina, MN 55439. Copyright © 2008 by Abdo Consulting Group, Inc. International copyrights reserved in all countries. No part of this book may be reproduced in any form without written permission from the publisher. Super SandCastle™ is a trademark and logo of ABDO Publishing Company.

Printed in the United States.

Editor: Pam Price
Curriculum Coordinator: Nancy Tuminelly
Cover and Interior Design and Production: Mighty Media

Library of Congress Cataloging-in-Publication Data

Freese, Susan M., 1958-
   Guppies to puppies : reading, writing, and reciting poems about pets /
   Susan M. Freese.
      p. cm. -- (Poetry power)
   Includes index.
   ISBN 978-1-60453-005-6
1. Poetry--Authorship--Juvenile literature. 2. Children's poetry, American.
3. Pets in literature. I. Title.

PN1059.A9F7435 2008
808.1--dc22
                        2007038001

Super SandCastle™ books are created by a team of professional educators, reading specialists, and content developers around five essential components—phonemic awareness, phonics, vocabulary, text comprehension, and fluency—to assist young readers as they develop reading skills and strategies and increase their general knowledge. All books are written, reviewed, and leveled for guided reading, early intervention reading, and Accelerated Reader® programs for use in shared, guided, and independent reading and writing activities to support a balanced approach to literacy instruction.

About SUPER SANDCASTLE™

Bigger Books for Emerging Readers
Grades PreK–3

Created for library, classroom, and at-home use, Super SandCastle™ books support and engage young readers as they develop and build literacy skills and will increase their general knowledge about the world around them. Super SandCastle™ books are part of SandCastle™, the leading preK–3 imprint for emerging and beginning readers. Super SandCastle™ features a larger trim size for more reading fun.

Let Us Know

Super SandCastle™ would like to hear your stories about reading this book. What was your favorite page? Was there something hard that you needed help with? Share the ups and downs of learning to read. We want to hear from you! Send us an e-mail.

sandcastle@abdopublishing.com

Contact us for a complete list of SandCastle™, Super SandCastle™, and other nonfiction and fiction titles from ABDO Publishing Company.
www.abdopublishing.com
8000 West 78th Street Edina, MN 55439
800-800-1312 · 952-831-1632 fax

A Note to Librarians, Teachers, and Parents

The poems in this book are grouped into three sections. "I Can Read" has poems that children can read on their own. "Read With Me" has poems that may require some reading help. "Kids' Corner" has poems written by children.

There are some words in these poems that young readers may not know. Some of these words are in boldface. Their pronunciations and definitions are given in the text. Other words can be looked up in the book's glossary.

When possible, children should first read each poem out loud. That way they will hear all of the sounds and feel all of the rhythms. If it is not possible to read aloud, instruct them to read the poems to themselves so they hear the words in their heads.

The **Poetry Pal** next to each poem explains how the poet uses words and specific styles or techniques to make the reader feel or know something.

The **Speak Up!** sidebar prompts readers to reflect on what they think each poem means and how it relates to them.

Become a Poet! provides ideas and activities to encourage and enhance learning about reading, writing, and reciting poetry.

Contents

what Is

Let's pretend someone has asked you to write about your favorite pet. Maybe that is your cat or your dog. But you have to follow these rules. First, you can't use very many words. And second, you have to put the words in order so they make a rhyme or a rhythm when you read them.

These are some of the rules for writing poetry. Poetry is different from the writing you do at school and other places, which is called **prose** (PROZE). Here's how!

Poets, the people who write poetry, use fewer words than other kinds of writers. That means they have to pick just the right words to say what they think and feel. The words in poems often are about how things look, feel, smell, taste, and sound. Poets use words to paint pictures for their readers.

poetry?

Poets also arrange words in ways to create rhyme and rhythm. You probably know that words that **rhyme** (RIME) sound the same, such as *cat*, *sat*, and *bat*. Rhyming words are fun to say and to hear. A **rhythm** (RIH-thum) is a pattern of sounds. Think about the beat you feel when you clap or march to music. You can feel the same kind of beat when you read a poem. By using rhythm and rhyme, poets make words sound like music.

What else is special about poetry? Because of all the choices poets get to make when they write, no two poems are ever the same. You will see that when you read the poems in this book! And you will find that out when you write your own poems too!

C
S
B
at

Getting Started

The terms on the next page tell how poets choose words and put them together in special ways. As you read about each term, look at the poem "Puppy Problem" to see an example.

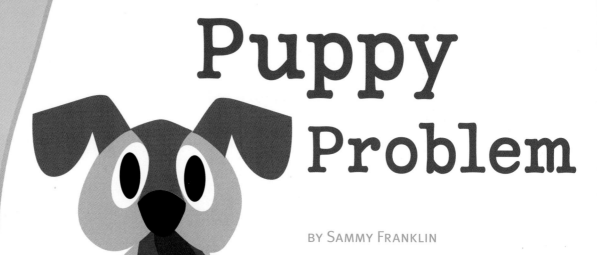

Puppy Problem

BY SAMMY FRANKLIN

I have a brand-new puppy,
Who likes to bite and chew.

Mother found him darling,
Until he ate her shoe!

line

A line in a poem is a group of words written across the page. In "Puppy Problem," the first line is "I have a brand-new puppy." Each new line starts below the one before it. There are four lines in this short poem.

stanza
(STAN-zuh)

A stanza is a group of lines in a poem that are usually about the same idea. A stanza is like a paragraph in other kinds of writing. Stanzas are separated by blank lines of space. "Puppy Problem" has two stanzas.

rhyme
(RIME)

Words that rhyme end with the same sound, such as *dog* and *log* and *fox* and *socks*. In a poem, the last words of the lines often rhyme but not always. In many poems, every pair of lines rhymes or every other line rhymes. In "Puppy Problem," lines 2 and 4 rhyme. They end with *chew* and *shoe*.

rhythm
(RIH-thum)

Even poems that don't rhyme have rhythm, a pattern of sounds or beats. In most poems, some sounds are accented. That means you say them with a little more punch. Read "Puppy Problem" aloud and listen to which sounds you accent. Clap on these sounds to help you hear and feel them. You probably read line 1 using a pattern like this, "I **HAVE** a **BRAND**-new **PUP**-py." To read this line, you accent every other sound, starting with the second one. Line 2 has the same pattern, and so do lines 3 and 4. All the lines in this poem have the same rhythm.

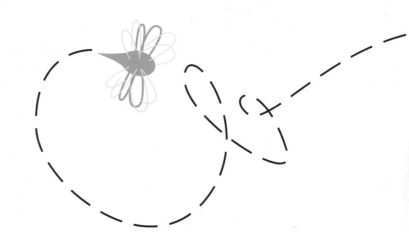

I Can Read

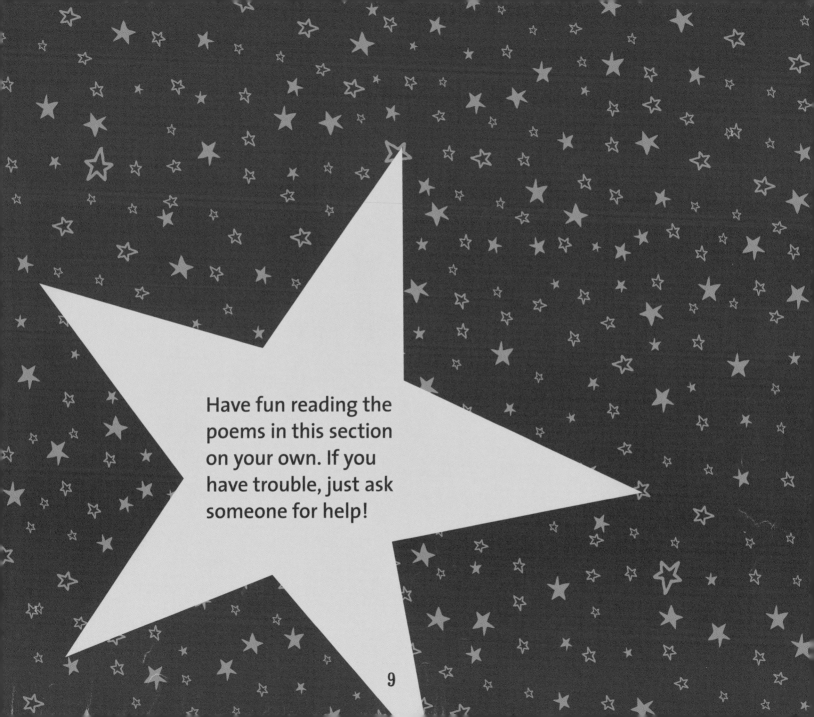

Have fun reading the poems in this section on your own. If you have trouble, just ask someone for help!

9

POETRY PAL

Compare the first two lines with the last two. They're the same! "Cats sleep anywhere" is the main idea, or **theme** (THEEM), of the poem. All the other lines tell the many places cats will sleep. This kind of list in a poem is called a **catalog** (CAT-uh-log).

Read this poem out loud. Listen to which lines you read quickly and slowly. Try starting slowly, speeding up, and then slowing down again. Take your time with the last four lines. Do you see the exclamation marks? Get excited! Also give the word *They* a little extra punch!

Cat!

BY ELEANOR FARJEON

Cats sleep
Anywhere,
Any table,
Any chair,
Top of piano,
Window-ledge,
In the middle,
On the edge,
Open drawer,
Empty shoe,

Anybody's
Lap will do,
Fitted in a
Cardboard box,
In the cupboard
With your frocks—
Anywhere!
They don't care!
Cats sleep
Anywhere.

Speak Up!

If you own a cat, than you know that cats mostly do what they want to do! Of all the places listed in the poem, where would you not want a cat to sleep? Why?

My Pony Is Recovering

BY LINDA KNAUS

My pony has been very ill,
with sneezing on and off.
He ran a low-grade fever, and
he had a nasty cough.

The virus left him very weak.
Although it's run its course,
my pony, as you might expect,
is still a little hoarse.

12

The Little Turtle

BY VACHEL LINDSAY

There was a little turtle.
He lived in a box.
He swam in a puddle.
He climbed on the rocks.

He snapped at a mosquito.
He snapped at a flea.
He snapped at a minnow.
And he snapped at me.

He caught the mosquito.
He caught the flea.
He caught the minnow.
But he didn't catch me.

POETRY PAL

This poem uses **repetition** (rep-uh-TIH-shun) by saying the same words over and over. This creates rhythm. In stanza 2, look for *He snapped*. In stanza 3, which words are repeated?

Poets also use repetition to show important ideas. What two ideas about the turtle are important?

SPEAK UP!

What are two important things about you? Why are they important?

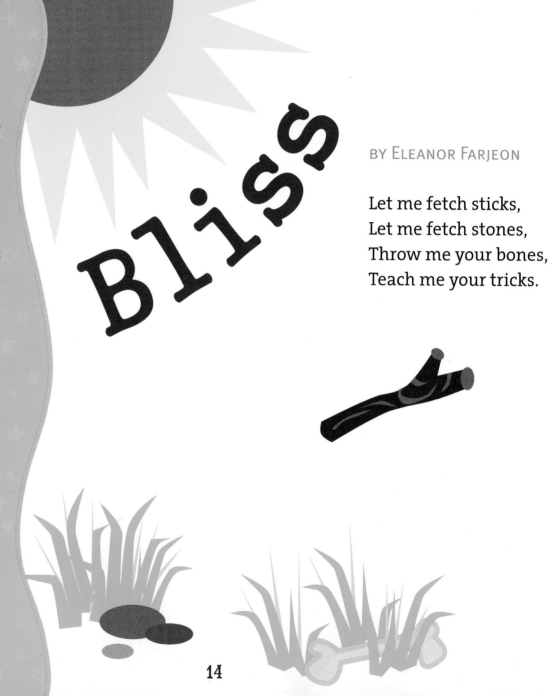

POETRY PAL

Who is "me" in this poem? You probably guessed after reading the first few lines that "me" is a dog. The dog is talking in this poem. This makes the dog the **speaker**. What clues helped you figure this out?

The dog is talking to its owner. What can you tell about the owner from what the dog says? How old is the owner? Look for clues in the poem.

Bliss

BY ELEANOR FARJEON

Let me fetch sticks,
Let me fetch stones,
Throw me your bones,
Teach me your tricks.

When you go ride,
Let me go run,
You in the sun,
Me at your side;

When you go swim,
Let me go too
Both lost in blue
Up to the brim;

Let me do this,
Let me do that—
What you are at,
That is my bliss.

SPEAK UP!

The title of this poem is "Bliss." What does *bliss* mean? Is it a good title? Why or why not?

POETRY PAL

The feeling a poem creates is called the **mood**. Think about how the mood changes in this poem. When you started reading, maybe you felt serious or even sad. But what did you find out in the last line? How did you feel then?

SPEAK UP!

When you're in a sad mood, what helps make you happy? Is there a person who can make you feel better? Do you find something fun to do or somewhere special to go?

My Goldfish

BY MARK BENTHALL

My goldfish died this morning
At exactly half past seven.

My mother helped me say a prayer
Then flushed him into heaven.

16

Cat Kisses

by Bobbi Katz

Sandpaper kisses
On a cheek or a chin —
That is the way
For a day to begin!

Sandpaper kisses —
A cuddle, a purr.
I have an alarm clock
That's covered with fur.

POETRY PAL

If you have ever been licked by a cat, then you know what *sandpaper kisses* feel like. Poets choose words that help readers see and feel and hear what they are talking about. These word pictures are called **images** (IM-uh-juz). What image forms in your mind after you read the last two lines?

SPEAK UP!

This poem is about having a cat wake you up in the morning. How do you like to wake up?

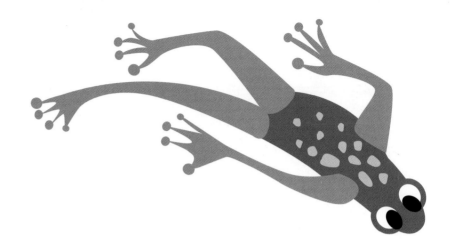

Read With Me

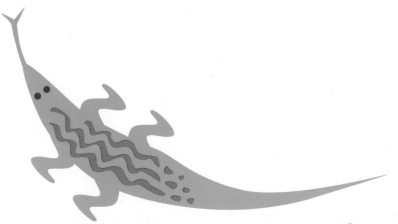

Enjoy reading these poems with someone who can help you with the harder words and ideas. Poetry is more fun when you understand what you are reading!

19

Two Little Kittens

Anonymous

Two little kittens, one stormy night,
Began to quarrel, and then to fight;
One had a mouse, the other had none,
And that's the way the quarrel begun.

"I'll have that mouse," said the biggest cat;
"You'll have that mouse? We'll see about that!"
"I will have that mouse," said the eldest son;
"You shan't have the mouse," said the little one.

20

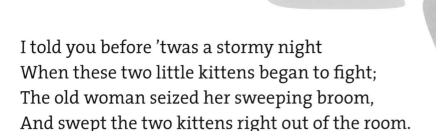

I told you before 'twas a stormy night
When these two little kittens began to fight;
The old woman seized her sweeping broom,
And swept the two kittens right out of the room.

The ground was covered with frost and snow,
And the two little kittens had nowhere to go;
So they laid them down on the mat at the door,
While the old woman finished sweeping the floor.

Then they crept in, as quiet as mice,
All wet with the snow, and cold as ice,
For they found it was better, that stormy night,
To lie down and sleep than to quarrel and fight.

SPEAK UP!

Many stories have a lesson to teach. That lesson is sometimes called the **moral** (MORE-ull) of the story. What lesson should readers learn from this narrative?

This poem helps you see and hear a dreaming dog. It uses **sensory details** (SEN-sore-ee DEE-tales), which tell how things look, sound, feel, taste, and smell. In the first stanza, what do the words *twitches*, *growls*, *whimpers*, *snarls*, and *yelps* tell you about the dog?

In the second stanza, the dog's dream seems to change. What is the dog dreaming about now?

SPEAK UP!

The first line says "Our sad old dog." Why do you think this dog is sad?

Dog Dreams

BY JANET S. WONG

Our sad old dog
kicks his feet,
twitches, growls
in his sleep,
whimpers, snarls,
yelps awake.

I scratch
behind his ears
and take him out
to let him sniff
the trees,
let him walk,
chase the breeze,
nose in air,
eyes closed tight,
chasing dreams
into the night.

Sunning

BY JAMES S. TIPPETT

Old Dog lay in the summer sun
Much too lazy to rise and run.
He flapped an ear
At a buzzing fly.
He winked a half opened
Sleepy eye.
He scratched himself
On an itching spot,
As he dozed on the porch
Where the sun was hot.
He whimpered a bit
From force of habit
While he lazily dreamed
Of chasing a rabbit.
But Old Dog happily lay in the sun
Much too lazy to rise and run.

23

POETRY PAL

This poem, like "Dog Dreams," uses sensory details to help you picture a dog in your mind. Where is the dog in this poem? What is it doing? List the sensory words that help you see and feel these things.

Like the dog in the other poem, this dog is dreaming. But what is it dreaming about? Is this dog having a good dream or a bad dream?

SPEAK UP!

The dog in this poem is old too. But is it sad, like the dog in the other poem?

Read the first two lines of the poem out loud. What do you notice? How many words begin with the letter *p*?

Now read the next two lines. What letters and sounds are repeated in them? When poets put together words that have the same beginning sound, they're using **alliteration** (uh-lit-er-A-shun).

What other examples of alliteration can you find in this poem?

Patricia Brought Her Parakeet

BY KENN NESBITT

Patricia brought her parakeet.
It pecked at Patrick's puppy.
Samantha's salamander swiftly
gobbled Gracie's guppy.

Savannah's snapping turtle
snapped the nose of Franklin's frog.
I'd say Fernando's ferret
went berserk on Daniel's dog.

Poor Jordan found his gerbil
being chased by Katelyn's cat,
and everyone was panicking
'cause Ryan brought his rat.

The teacher screamed and fainted,
and she fell right off her stool.
I guess I shouldn't bring
my pet tarantula to school.

She soon enough recovered,
but you should have heard her yell.
It looks like that's the last time
we'll bring pets for show-and-tell.

SPEAK UP!

What kinds of pets start
with the same sound as your
name? For instance, the name
Matthew can be matched with
monkey and *mouse*. Find two kinds of
pets for your name. They can be real or
pretend kinds of pets. Be creative!

25

This is a **list poem**. It has two parts, a subject and a list of words about the subject. The subject here is "The cat," and the words in the list tell what the cat is doing.

To write your own list poem about a cat, you could use words that say what a cat looks like, such as *white*, *furry*, and so on.

The Cat

BY AMY DRUMMOND

The cat
    sleeping
    playing
    purring
    licking
    eating
    stretching
    scratching

26

Five Little Puppies

BY STEVEN FULLER

Five little puppies
Jumping on the door,
One pushed it open
And then there were four.

Four little puppies
Running 'round the tree,
One chased a squirrel
And then there were three.

Three little puppies
Tugging on a shoe,
One got stuck inside it
And then there were two.

Two little puppies
Laying in the sun,
One fell asleep
And then there was one.

One little puppy
Sad to be alone,
Dug into the garden
And found a great big bone.

27

POETRY PAL

This is a **counting poem**, and it follows a set pattern. You can write your own counting poem in your poetry journal. To begin, pick a subject to fill in this line, "Five little _____." The first line of every stanza is like this, except the number goes down by one each time.

Something else that's the same in each stanza is that lines 2 and 4 rhyme. To pick rhyming words for these lines, start with line 4. It has to end in a word that's a number.

What other patterns do you see?

Become a Poet!

Here are some activities to help you write your own poems.

Keep a Journal

Many writers keep a journal, which is a book of ideas, thoughts and drawings. Start your own journal in an empty notebook. Write down ideas for your own poems. Write down things that happen, what you like and don't like. Keep your journal with you so you can use it often.

Learn New Words

In the back of your journal, make a list of new words you learn. Start with the words you learned while reading the poems in this book. Write down each word and what it means. Then write each word in a sentence to make sure you know how to use it. Also write down how to say it if you think you won't remember.

Make a Picture

Draw or paint a picture about one of the poems in this book. Maybe pick one of the poems that has many words about colors and other things you can see. Share both the poem and the picture with someone.

Write a Story

Choose one of the poems in this book and write a story from it. Your story can be about what's happening in the poem or who's in the poem. Write using your own words, not the words from the poem.

Have a Poetry Reading

With a few friends or family members, put on a show where everyone has a turn to read a poem out loud. When people aren't reading, they should be in the audience. Practice using correct rhythm and rhyme beforehand. Also make sure you know all the words. Try reciting the poem from memory, if you can.

Find More Poems

What's your favorite poem in this book? Who wrote it? Use the Internet and books in your library to find another poem by this poet. Read the new poem several times. Then read your favorite poem again. How are the two poems alike? How are they different? Which poem do you like best now? Write about the poems in your journal.

Learn About Poets

Use the Internet or books in your library to learn about famous poets. Start with Eleanor Farjeon, who writes a lot of children's poems. Where is she from? What poems has she written? Read four poems by Eleanor Farjeon and pick your favorite. Write down in your journal why you like this poem the best.

Make a Recording

Record yourself reading one of the poems from this book out loud. Practice so you can read the poem with the correct rhythm and rhyme. Ask your parent or teacher for help, if you need it. Record other poems later to make a set of your favorite poems.

Glossary

berserk – crazy or wild.

bliss – complete happiness.

brim – the upper or outer edge of a container.

fetch – to go after something and bring it back.

frock – a dress.

hoarse – having a rough or harsh-sounding voice.

panic – to become very frightened and maybe even out of control.

quarrel – to have an angry dispute or argument.

seize – to grab or take something.

permissions

Index